The Korean Martial Art of Self Defense

HAP KI DO

By Master Choe

Practical Hap Ki Do Textbook

For information address:
World Hapkido Association
1789 Thousand Oaks Blvd. • Thousand Oaks, Ca 91360 • USA

To contact Master Choe, or order additional copies of this book:
e-mail: masterchoe@worldhapkido.com
Website: worldhapkido.com
ISBN#0-966825411
U.S. Library of Congress Control # 2002117352

Technique photographs by Clemente Photography
Cover and book design by Chito PeBenito - CHiTO Graphic & Design

Other Master Choe's books you will enjoy:

VOLUME I (Basic Techniques) Hap Ki Do - The Korean Martial Art
(ISBN# 0-9668254-0-3)
A fully illustrated book on the Martial Art of Hap Ki Do. Filled with over 400 photographs. Designed to show Hap Ki Do in an easy to follow step by step methods for beginners. Included are close up photos of various wristlocks, arrow to show certain steps and minimal wording on the steps, to make this book easy to follow.

VOLUME III Hap Ki Do: A Guide to Black Belt Studies
(ISBN# 0-9668254-4-6)
Teacher, Warrior, Master Choe continues his outstanding series of books on the Korean Martial Art of Hap Ki Do. Hap Ki Do is a discipline of coordination, a way of strengthening the mind and body, of fusing the individuals physical and mental powers so that he or she will emerge as a more fully integrated human being. Master Choe has beautifully intertwined theory and philosophy along with basic and advanced self defense techniques in this third book Hap Ki Do: A Guide to Black Belt Studies. Over 400 photographs of unparalleled clarity and rich text illustrating joint lock, throwing and finishing techniques. Realizing the student studying to be a black belt is eager to learn the many techniques to test for Black Belt master Choe turns his focus on the theory and philosophy of Hap Ki Do suggesting to the student to think and establish a martial moral philosophy as well as practicing Hap Ki Do techniques. The student of martial arts or student of like will relish in every work of wisdom that takes them to a deeper understanding of their own style and moral philosophy.

Hap Ki Do - Instructional Video
(ISBN# 0-9668254-3-8)
This is an excellent source for Hap Ki Do students or students of martial arts. This video is an excellent source to go along with Master Choe's "Practical Hap Ki Do Textbook".
20 minutes, VHS

Coming Soon: VOLUME IV (Hap Ki Do - Kicking and Sparring Techniques)

For the LORD gives wisdom, and from his mouth come knowledge and understanding.

Proverbs 2:6

-FOREWORD-

I wrote this and my previous Hap Ki Do book because there are very few books written about the Korean Martial Art of Hap Ki Do. I also want to share my knowledge of Hap Ki Do with my current students, potential students, and martial arts practitioners who want to learn about Hap Ki Do.

Although my goal is to share my knowledge and help develop the versatile art of Hap Ki Do, I feel that it is important to establish that martial arts are not only about the physical skill. In order to be a true martial artist, you must condition your mind as well as your body. The Chinese philosopher, Sun Tzu wrote that a person, who knows when to fight and when not to fight, would always win. He also wrote about achieving success through knowing yourself and your enemy. Man's greatest enemy is fear, martial artists, whether they are Hap Ki Do stylist or not, must acknowledge their fears and fight to overcome them in order to succeed. This will result in a calm clear mind, and like a clear empty sky you will experience tranquillity and a healthy mind and body.

There are many lessons to be learned when dealing with the philosophical aspects of the martial arts. I have studied a variety of arts and read dozens of books about the philosophy and meaning behind the arts. The more I read, the more I learned about the true secrets such as honor, integrity, kindness, patience, self confidence and many other positive traits. I encourage you to practice your skills and open your minds to the knowledge and great possibilities that await you.

Master Hui S Choe - About the Author

Master Choe (Pronounced CHAY) Hui Son. Born and raised in Seoul, Korea he began his Martial Arts studies at the age of 6. He studied both Tae Kwon Do and Hap Ki Do. Master Choe received his 1st Dan Black Belt in Tae Kwon Do from Supreme Grand Master Ko at the age of 9. Master Choe currently holds a certified 6th Dan in Tae Kwon Do. He received his 1st Dan Black Belt in Hap Ki Do at the age of 13 from Grand Master Yoon, Byoung Ok. Master Choe is a certified 7th Dan Hap Ki Do.

While in high school Master Choe expanded his Martial Arts knowledge by studying Shaolin Kung Fu. He continued to improve his ability and knowledge in Hap Ki Do and Tae Kwon Do as well. He also learned the philosophy of Kendo from Grandmaster Omoto in the USA.

In 1980 Master Choe became the head instructor for the U.S. Army at Camp Stanley in South Korea. He later served his country when he became a Marine in the South Korean Marine Corps. After Master Choe finished his tour in the military, he opened his own Hap Ki Do Martial Arts School in Seoul. In 1987, Master Choe was asked to serve his country again as a personal bodyguard for the South Korean Prime Minister, Kim, Jong Pil. In 1988 Master Choe became one of the training staff for the South Korean Olympic Power Lifting Team.

In 1989 Master Choe moved to the United States and opened Choe's Hap Ki Do School in Spanaway, Washington State. In 1999 Master Choe opened another Hap Ki Do School in Federal Way, WA. He also teaches Hap Ki Do to the Military people in Fort Lewis, Washington.

Master Choe currently is the President of WORLD HAP KI DO ASSOCIATION.

- 7th Degree Black Belt in Hap Ki Do
- 6th Degree Black Belt in Tae Kwon Do
- Appointed as Instructor of Kum-Moo-Kwan Do Jang in Korea Hapkido Association
- Appointed to teach Martial Arts to Fort Lewis Military Personnel
- Author of Basic Hap Ki Do
- Video Hap KI Do Basic 1/Hap Ki Do Advanced 2
- Registered Master in Hap Ki Do and Tae Kwon Do in Washington State, USA

-TABLE OF CONTENTS-

Teaching the Martial Art Philosophy to the American People.

I have been teaching Jeon-Tong-Moo-Sul (Traditional martial arts) to American students since 1990. As soon as I started to teach the martial arts to them, I found that I also had to teach Oriental philosophy to complete their understanding.

However, at the time my English was poor and my ability to make them understand was limited. The martial arts try to harmonize the mind and the body, but I could only teach them the techniques. It was comparable to teaching how to play football without the ball. Then I began to study hard to learn the English language and figured out how to teach my students the necessary philosophy. I always begin my class by having the students sit down, close their eyes and concentrate on their breathing. After a few minutes, I order them to relax and clear their mind like an empty sky. There is no fear or stress, only peace. The children obviously have a harder time with this than the adults. They do; however, adapt quickly.

Nobody knows anything before they are born. You can only learn the necessities in life one by one, day by day. My joy comes from teaching them with an example of my life and an indomitable spirit that comes from inner peace.

Practicing the Martial Arts

Normally, there is between 20-30 students per class. There are various types of students with various attitudes. The more diligent ones prepare before class. They practice their techniques and are ready to learn more. The less organized show up late, never practice and seem to get frustrated because they can't remember what they need to know. The more athletic students usually learn their techniques faster, but they still need to practice to be able to remember them in a real situation. No matter what, there are no short cuts when learning the martial arts. The usual dropouts are the impatient. In the martial arts, you must try to learn not only the physical but also the emotional and the spiritual, which often takes far longer to achieve. Keeping up your physique is essential to martial arts Instructor or Master. They should always be the epitome of flexibility and strength as to inspire the student to achieve the same. Some Instructors or Masters stop their training which translates to uninspired students. It was not like that long ago. Masters would continue their training until late in life. The learning over that long a period of time would go beyond just techniques rather it would be a road to enlightenment or a Zen (no will) motion. You can find that Zen motion in anything you do for such a long time and repetitive manner. A long time ago, a famous Butcher in Korea could cut a cow unbelievably quick and efficiently. In his mind was a template of where the cow's bones were located and he would make his cuts quick and precise. The martial art training is the same. You must repeat everything endlessly to understand that simple things are not so simple. The more you understand the more complicated it becomes. The more you practice the less will behind your actions.

-CONCEPTS-

Kyoung-Rae (bow) - Respect in the Martial Arts

Martial artists learn how to show respect to their master by bowing. They often continue to show respect to their friends and family in the same manner. The bow is the best way to show their attitude, respect and loyalty. That is why the bow is serious and solemn. You can bow from a standing position or from a kneeling position. The standing bow is used to replace the common handshake that Americans use. A proper bow begins by putting your feet together and bending forward 30 degree from the waist. Keep your hands open and at your thighs. You should see the person's feet when bowing. The bow is used when entering important places such as the Do-jang. The student should seek the Master and bow to him respectfully first. The martial artist also bows to their practice partners before and after practicing together. Along with maintaining respect, the bow focuses your mind and body. A kneeling bow is a ceremonial greeting. You must perform a kneeling bow before starting and after finishing the class. It is used when showing high reverence to someone. For example a senior citizen who holds an important position to you. When performing a kneeling bow you place your palms on the ground in front of you and bring your forehead down to the back of your hands. Don't raise your hips when bending forward. This requires sufficient flexibility in the knees. It will be difficult for people unaccustomed to kneeling.

Ho-Shin-Sool (Self Defense)

Hapkido Ho-shin-sool consists of striking, joint-locks and throwing techniques. The attack or defense you use often depends on the distance between you and the opponent. There are two main types of attack. One is a strike with the hands and feet, and the other is grab or hold. It is a simple concept as to when to use your feet instead of your hands. If you can reach the opponent with your feet but not your hands, you would kick. If you are closer, your kicks become less effective than your hands, so you strike with your hands. When you are even closer, you are in contact with your opponent in a hold or grab. Punching and striking become less effective than a throw or joint-lock. By twisting and turning you can free yourself and attack your opponent's joints (wrist, elbow, finger, shoulder, neck, ankle etc.) with techniques such as Hei-jun, Boo-chae, Yun-hang, and Pal-kum-chi. A more deadly counter attack is Mok-jo-ru-gi (choke). When you are this close Dun-ji-gi (throwing technique) can also be used very effectively. Many techniques don't require much strength since you use your opponent's strength against him. You can then break his balance easily by using hand throws, leg throws, and body throws similar to Judo.

Focus in the Training

A strong focus is a very important point that allows you to decipher your opponent's movement easily when you engage him. Looking at your opponent's whole body gives you some ideas about his next action and which leg or arm he is going to use. You have to watch him very carefully. Most students just look at their opponent's feet because they only worry about their opponent's kicks. However, it's a big mistake to do that as the feet can be used to deceive you through footwork. If you focused on World Champion Boxer, Sugar Ray Leonard's feet you would not last to see the second round. If you only use a narrow focus of judgement, you will not be able to defend yourself effectively.

Since martial arts began, many masters like to look at their opponents with a wide view that takes in the opponent from head to foot even though their eyes focus on the opponent's eyes. Only then, can they see the opponent's position and balance, thus, guess the opponent's next actions. It's like a chess game. You have to know the opponent's mind and will through his eyes so that you can prepare to attack or defend. The eyes will tell you how ready he is to attack or how ready he is to run. Your techniques will depend on how he prepares his feet. For example, if your opponent takes a left side stance, (Puts his left foot forward) he likes to use his left leg for defense and to use his right leg for offense because of the balance. As a result, to anticipate your opponent's "next move" is the key that often decides whether you win or lose.

Distance

A distance between you and your opponent decides your reaction (Self-defense) against his/her attacks. To keep a safe distance gives you a clear vision to prepare an unexpected attack. When you stand close your opponent, you can't see their whole body with your vision so that it makes you hard to prepare their attack. Thus, I like to tell my students to keep three steps far away from their opponents because you can see their movement so clearly before they attacks. In a short distance, the opponent never gives you time to defend their attack. For example, when you stand one step away from your opponent, they can attack you with their legs and arms easily. Two steps away, they can reach you with just their legs. Therefore, I think the three steps distance is a safety zone, but your opponent can attack you with their step, so you have to keep your safe distance from your attacker. Most martial artists move their bodies with some steps: moving forward, backward and side way, when they attack their opponents, so it makes their opponents confuse to estimate the distance. To move step also make hard to hit a target for the attacker because of an unsettled target; consequently, many martial artists practice to punch and kick a moving sandbag instead of an opponent

Kyuk-pa - The Art of Breaking Boards and Bricks

People always find it exciting to watch Martial Arts demonstration. Usually the most exciting part is watching a martial artist break boards or bricks. For the martial artist doing the break it is important to consider three very important points. Balance, strong power and conditioning, and true confidence. You must keep good balance to deliver power and to maintain power through the break. When you stand in front of a target to do a break, you must position yourself for maximum power. Your left foot, right foot, and the target must form a triangle. The triangle is the strongest geometric form. This also allows you the most comfortable striking position. Your Dan-jun power can be used to assist your break since it is the center of your gravity. This position allows you to project your center of gravity through the board or brick.

Your actual power comes from many years of technical practice. When you learn any form of striking you practice hard to correct the motion. You then practice long to develop the strength in the appropriate areas. Finally you practice the longest to develop the relaxed state that gives you maximum speed and timing before impact. You must be flexed at the point of impact but relaxed just before and after. This timing gives you the "knock out" power in your hands and feet. Putting your weight behind the strike is also important. Power is the product of speed and mass according to the laws of physics. This is why a small person can have power because of speed and a large person can have power because of weight. This is the same reason a large person who doesn't have speed and does not know how to put their weight behind the strike has little power.

Once you deliver the power you must be properly conditioned. You can deliver tremendous power with a hammer onto a nail but the hammer will surely break if it is made of plastic. Your hands and feet require a hardening through many years of hitting hard surfaces. These hard surfaces can be wooden targets or punching bags, which will cause the thickening of the skin. The skin can then act like a cushion during impact to prevent trauma to the underlying bones. Probably the most important factor is the developing of the right mind set.

True confidence is required to release maximum power. Your mind can defeat you long before you try to break a board or a brick even though your physical state is more than able to accomplish the task. You must break the board or brick by using the philosophy of the martial arts. You must use your mind, body, and spirit completely! Take into consideration that even though I have trained for many years and have successfully broken many boards and bricks, sometimes the board or brick wins.

The Exercise of Concentration

In the martial arts, concentration is very important. You can concentrate your mind on gathering innumerable power from your source. This source is believed to be your center or Dan-jun located three fingers below your navel. This is Ki. It takes many years to master the ability to draw this Ki power. With the proper guidance from your master, it takes very little time to realize its existence. Through your continued concentration you can reach Zen. This can also be referred to as a meditative state. In the East, many Buddhist Temples and Martial Art Do-jangs pursue Zen. This is an endless pursuit. The use of meditation is common. When you are seated comfortably and relaxed, you may begin your breathing exercises. Inhalation through the nose is a long controlled thin stream of air drawn down to your Dan-jun. The sound of this inhalation should resemble the letter "u". It should be relaxed and without strain. Since you are imaging drawing your air beyond your lungs to your lower abdomen let the abdomen expand at the same time as your lungs. Don't strain your stomach muscles. The idea is to breathe just like a sleeping baby fully and naturally. Keep your shoulders relaxed and down during inhalation. Exhalation is done through your mouth at the same rate as inhalation. Meditation is meant to discover calm and to centralize yourself as you quest for the same in your daily life. Proper breathing is the key. Many Martial Art practitioners declare that without proper breathing, the progress will always be limited. Hapkido means "to harmonize your inner and outer power". If you can gather power from your Dan-jun (Ki center) you are then able to mix it with your outer power. This is called universal energy. When a beginner martial artist engages a martial artist who has developed a strong Ki, the results are usually the same. Often the beginner cannot move as he expects because the stronger Ki suppresses the weaker Ki on the universal playing field. This results in the beginner losing their will to fight.

Concept of Defense

There are various forms or techniques in the martial arts. Some are designed for self-defense such as Hapkido techniques. I define the main elements of self-defense as correct observation and a rapid circular motion (Hei-jun). While you are engaging with your opponent, a good observation will clearly show their intention to you. You must check what kind of posture they have, where their main balance is and what the condition of his/her breathing. If your opponent stands on the left or right side posture (Fighting stance), you assume the kind of techniques you have to use when they attack. Glancing at your opponent's balance, you will find special features that distinguish a beginner from a professional fighter. In the animal kingdom it would be comparable to determining if the animal is a predator or prey. There are some obvious signs. For example, the beginner always has an unstable balance so it is easy to handle them. It is, however, extremely difficult to find out the professional fighter's balance because of their deceptive posture. Through correct observation of your opponent breath, you can determine if they are tired or nervous. However, if your opponent has a calm breath just like a quite ocean, they must have a strong ki (Inner energy).

A circular motion (Hei-jun) is very important in hapkido techniques. The circle is continuous on the same spot. Unlike a straight line, you need to travel to keep continuous. The ability to keep flowing from one technique to another is what makes hapkido so effective. To practice, we turn our direction as much as we can during the techniques even though we still use many powerful straight punches and kicks. There are three circular movements: Dwi-ro-do-ra, turn without step; Ban-hei-jun, half turn with one step; Hei-jun, full turn with two steps. These movements lead your opponent to lose their target (you) and lose their balance. This movement is the "float like a butterfly, sting like a bee" that made Muhamed Ali so difficult to hit! Yet he could strike at will with a strong straight punch.

KI-BON-MAK-KI

Basic Blocking

Left Inside Out Block

KI-BON-MAK-KI - LEFT INSIDE OUT BLOCK

1

Technique 1

1. Attacker faces you in a fighting stance. You are in a ready stance.

2. Attacker punches with his right hand. You left inside out block and right hand.

3. Punch to the attacker's solar plexus.

2

3

Technique 2

1. Attacker faces you in a fighting stance. You are in a ready stance.

2. Attacker punches with his right hand. You left inside out block and right hand punch to the attacker's solar plexus.

3. Finish striking with a right leg turn kick.

1

2

3

KI-BON-MAK-KI - LEFT INSIDE OUT BLOCK

1

Technique 3

1. Attacker faces you in a fighting stance. You are in a ready stance.
2. Attacker punches with his right hand. You left inside out block and right hand punch to the attacker's solar plexus.
3. Grab the attacker's right wrist your left hand. Grab the attacker's right shoulder with your right hand.
4. Step your right leg behind attacker's right leg.
5. Pull towards you and push the attacker's shoulder over until the attacker falls to the ground.

2

4

3

5

KI-BON-MAK-KI - LEFT INSIDE OUT BLOCK

Technique 4

1. Attacker faces you in a fighting stance. You are in a ready stance.

2. Attacker punches with his right hand. You left inside out block and right hand punch to the attacker's solar plexus.

3. Pull attacker's punch across the front of your body with both hands.

Continued on Next Page.

KI-BON-MAK-KI - LEFT INSIDE OUT BLOCK

4

Continued from page 17

4. Continue the motion while stepping across with your left foot. Begin raising the attacker's hand in the process.

5. Bring the attacker's hand over your head as you turn 180∞ clockwise. Your hold will begin bending the attacker's wrist into a painful lock.

6. The attacker will be thrown to the ground by continuing the motion.

5

6

KI-BON-MAK-KI - LEFT INSIDE OUT BLOCK

1

Technique 5

1. Attacker faces you in a fighting stance. You are in a ready stance.
2. Attacker punches with his right hand. You left inside out block and right hand punch to the attacker's solar plexus.
3. Grab the attacker's right wrist with your left. Place your right hand on attacker's left side of head.
4. Pivoting on your right foot turn 180∞ bringing attacker's arm with you and pushing downward on attacker's head with your right hand.
5. As you continue the motion the attacker will be forced to the ground.

2

3

4

5

Master Choe

KI-BON-MAK-KI

Basic Blocking

Right Inside Out Block

1

2

3

Technique 1

1. Attacker faces you in a fighting stance. You are in a ready stance.

2. Attacker punches with his right hand. You right inside out block to the outside of his right hand.

3. Strike with a left hand punch to the attacker's rib cage.

KI-BON-MAK-KI - RIGHT INSIDE OUT BLOCK

Technique 2

1. Attacker faces you in a fighting stance. You are in a ready stance.

2. Attacker punches with his right hand. You right inside out block to the outside of his right hand. Grab attacker's right wrist and strike with a left hand punch to the attacker's rib cage.

3. Finish striking with a left leg turn kick to the attacker's rib cage while still holding his right wrist.

KI-BON-MAK-KI - RIGHT INSIDE OUT BLOCK

1

2

3

Technique 3

1. Attacker faces you in a fighting stance. You are in a ready stance.

2. Attacker punches with his right hand. You right inside out block to the outside of his right hand.Grab attacker's right wrist and strike with a left hand punch to the attacker's rib cage.

3. Place your left hand across attackers elbow for a pal-kum-chi technique.

4. Continue to hyper extend the attacker's right elbow until he is forced to the ground.

4

KI-BON-MAK-KI - RIGHT INSIDE OUT BLOCK

1

Technique 4

1. Attacker faces you in a fighting stance. You are in a ready stance.
2. Attacker punches with his right hand. You right inside out block to the outside of his right hand. Grab attacker's right wrist and strike with a left hand punch to the attacker's rib cage.
3. Grab (fingers over) attacker's right elbow.
4. Bend his elbow by pulling on it and pushing his right hand forward and over his shoulder with your right hand.
5. This motion will take him to the ground where you can maintain the pressure. You do this by now pulling on his right wrist skyward. Always keep his elbow above his wrist to form a tight bend in his arm.

2

3

4

5

KI-BON-MAK-KI - RIGHT INSIDE OUT BLOCK

Technique 5

1. Attacker faces you in a fighting stance. You are in a ready stance.

2. Attacker punches with his right hand. You right inside out block to the outside of his right hand. Grab attacker's right wrist and strike with a left hand punch to the attacker's rib cage.

3. Bring your left hand over his shoulder and place the edge of your hand against his throat.

KI-BON-MAK-KI - RIGHT INSIDE OUT BLOCK

4. Sweep the attacker's right leg with your left leg as you continue to apply pressure on attacker's throat (4a). This will throw the attacker to the ground (4b).

4

4a

4b

Master Choe Jumping Side Kick

KI-BON-MAK-KI

Basic Blocking

Right Middle Block

KI-BON-MAK-KI - RIGHT MIDDLE BLOCK

Technique 1

1. Attacker faces you in a fighting stance. You are in a ready stance.

2. Step forward with your right leg and middle block attacker's right punch at the inside wrist.

3. Follow through into a back fist to the attacker's right temple.

KI-BON-MAK-KI - RIGHT MIDDLE BLOCK

1

Technique 2

1. Attacker faces you in a fighting stance. You are in a ready stance.

2. Step forward with your right leg and middle block attacker's right punch at the inside wrist.

3. Follow through into a back fist to the attacker's right temple.

4. Finish striking with a left hand punch to the attacker's rib cage.

2

3

4

KI-BON-MAK-KI - RIGHT MIDDLE BLOCK

1

Technique 3

1. Attacker faces you in a fighting stance. You are in a ready stance.
2. Step forward with your right leg and middle block attacker's right punch at the inside wrist.
3. Grab attacker's right back hand with your right hand.
4. Turn attacker's wrist over clockwise and bend back as you deliver a right leg turn kick to attacker's mid section.
5. Double up your grip on attacker's right hand and apply more pressure.

2

4

3

5

KI-BON-MAK-KI - RIGHT MIDDLE BLOCK

1

Technique 4

1. Attacker faces you in a fighting stance. You are in a ready stance.
2. Step forward with your right leg and middle block attacker's right punch at the inside wrist. Grab(fingers over) attacker's right punch with your left hand immediately following the block.
3. Drop your right hand under the attacker's right arm and deliver a back fist to his rib cage.
4. Hook your right arm under attacker's right arm as you step close with your right foot. Pivot on the right foot as you crouch and turn 180∞ with your left foot. You will have both your feet on the inside of attacker's feet.
5. Pull the attacker close as you bend and lift with your legs. A slight twist during this motion will throw the attacker over your hip.

2

3

4

5

KI-BON-MAK-KI - RIGHT MIDDLE BLOCK

Technique 5

1. Attacker faces you in a fighting stance. You are in a ready stance. Step forward with your right leg and middle block attacker's right punch at the inside wrist.

2. Strike the attacker on the right temple with a back fist.

3. Reach over and slide your arm in until attacker's head is by your under arm.

KI-BON-MAK-KI - RIGHT MIDDLE BLOCK

4. Hook your arm under attacker's chin so that your forearm is across his throat.

5. Drop down to your seat and lift the attacker over your head by placing your right leg on the inside of attacker's left leg as you roll onto your back.

6. The attacker will end up head to head with you as you continue to apply a choke hold with your forearm.

6

5

4

Master Choe, Instructor Chris and Black Belt Students

KI-BON-MAK-KI

Basic Blocking

Left Middle Block

KI-BON-MAK-KI - LEFT MIDDLE BLOCK

Technique 1

1. Attacker faces you in a fighting stance. You are in a ready stance.

2. Step forward with your left leg and middle block attacker's right punch at the outside wrist.

3. Follow through with a right elbow strike to the attacker's rib cage.

KI-BON-MAK-KI - LEFT MIDDLE BLOCK

1

2

3

Technique 2

1. Attacker faces you in a fighting stance. You are in a ready stance.

2. Step forward with your left leg and middle block attacker's right punch at the outside wrist.

3. Follow through with a right elbow strike to the attacker's rib cage.

4. Straighten your right arm to slip it over and the attacker's upper shoulders. Pull him down as you deliver a right knee strike to his mid section.

4

KI-BON-MAK-KI - LEFT MIDDLE BLOCK

1

Technique 3

1. Attacker faces you in a fighting stance. You are in a ready stance.

2. Step forward with your left leg and middle block attacker's right punch at the outside wrist.

3. Right hand comes under to grab the attackers right wrist. Your left hand opens and joins your right hand to double up your grip on his right wrist.

4. Swing your left elbow across and over his right arm as your left leg steps across and under his right arm. Tuck his arm under yours. Bring his shoulder down to your left knee as you lift his hand skyward.

2

3

4

Technique 4

1. Attacker faces you in a fighting stance. You are in a ready stance.
2. Step forward with your left leg and middle block attacker's right punch at the outside wrist.
3. Open your left hand to grab(fingers over) attacker's right wrist. Deliver a right hand strike to attacker's rib cage.
4. Double up your hold on attacker's right wrist. Turn attacker's wrist back and over(Boo-chae).
5. When the attacker is on the ground step forward and place your right knee down on his chest while continuing the pressure on his wrist.

1

2

3

4

5

1

2

3

Technique 5

1. Attacker faces you in a fighting stance. You are in a ready stance.

2. Step forward with your left leg and middle block attacker's right punch at the outside wrist.

3. Swing your right arm up and forward until your right shoulder is at his underarm. Your left hand is reaching behind his back to meet your right hand.

4. Once your hands meet squeeze towards your chest as you push forwards with your right shoulder. Keep your head tucked away so it can't be reached with his arms or a head bunt. This will choke the attacker.

4

BASIC KICKS

Master Choe - jumping side kick

1

Instep groin kick

1. Stand with your left leg forward. Legs apart and slightly bent. Shoulders are sideways to the direction you are going to kick.

2. Bring your weight forward onto your left leg as you lift your right knee up and forward.

3. Extend your right leg in a snapping motion out and back. Lean slightly back to allow your reach to extend forward.

2

3

4

5

6

4. When your distance is farther than your arm reach you can deliver this fast kick.

5. Make sure your knee is slightly higher than the final target as you want to extend through the target.

6. Deliver the "snap" and finish by stepping down to a kicking stance again.

Sweeping kick

1. Stand with your left leg forward. Legs apart and slightly bent. Shoulders are sideways to the direction you are going to kick.

2. Turn your knee slightly to the outside as you begin to extend your right heel forward.

3. Thrust your heel forward until your leg extends. Lean back slightly to enable you to reach farther.

4. You must pull back your foot and toes to allow the heel to extend forward.

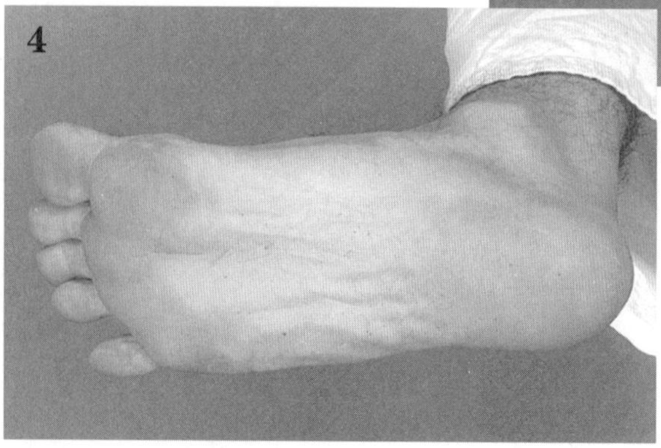

5

6

7

5. The low heel kick is an effective knee attack. It begins with your kicking stance position.

6. Raise your right heel to your left knee.

7. Extend your leg thrusting your heel to the attacker's front knee.

Front kick

1. Front kick begins in a proper kicking stance as always.

2. Bring the right knee high and forward.

3. Extend the leg with a snapping motion high in front.

4. Kick with the ball of your foot. You achieve this by extending your foot and pulling back your toes.

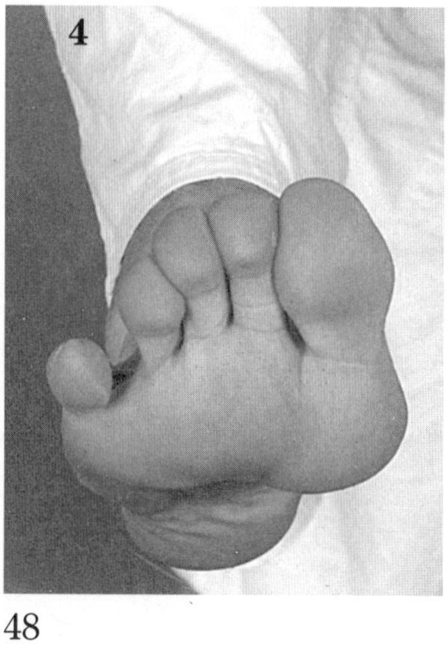

5

6

7

5. You are facing an attacker in a kicking stance.

6. Square your hips and drive your knee toward the attacker's mid-section. Make sure you keep your foot tucked close to your leg.

7. Extend leg forward thrusting the ball of your foot into the attacker's mid-section.

Push kick

1. Pushing kick begins from your kicking stance.

2. Lift knee to your chest bending your leg about 90°. This will place your foot in front of you. Pull your foot back to expose the bottom. Your standing foot will have turned slightly to allow your hips to rotate.

3. Extend your leg in a horizontal push turning your standing foot more as you reach out. This will make your body turn sideways at full extension.

1

2

3

4

5

6

4. Face your opponent in a kicking stance.

5. Lift your knee to your chest as you lunge towards him.

6. Place the foot on his chest with your knee bent. You can now extend your leg pushing him back with great force as your momen tum and weight are falling towards him.

BASIC KICKS • SIDE KICK

Side kick

1. Stand ready to deliver a side kick.

2. Bring your right knee parallel to the floor.

3. Pivot on your left foot to turn your body sideways.

4. Thrust your heel forward until your leg is fully extended.

5. Face opponent with a kicking stance.

6. Bring your knee up until it is be tween you and your opponent.

6a. You must strike with a foot knife. Your foot and toes are pulled back. Extend the outside edge of your foot. The edge and your heel make up the striking area.

3

4

6

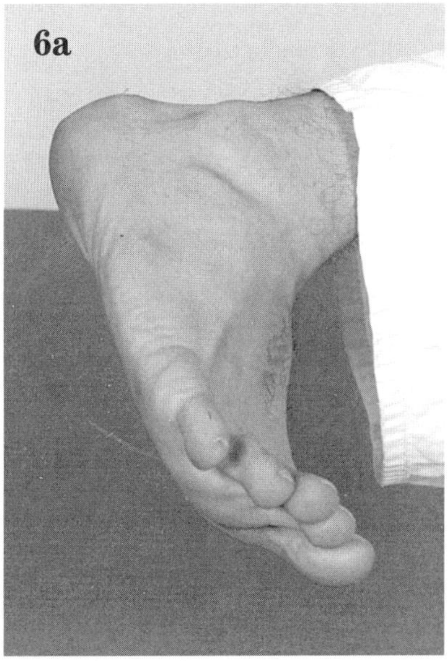
6a

7. You can sidekick high ...
8. midsection ...
9. or low...

7

8

9

Low Side Kick

1. Ready to deliver a low side kick.

2. Chamber up your knee to sideways kicking position.

3. To extend your reach you will have to bend your standing leg. Balance yourself by leaning forward and backwards as required. Your standing foot must pivot enough to all the necessary hip rotation.

1

2

3

1

2

Roundhouse Kick
1. Stand ready to deliver a roundhouse kick.

2. Bring your knee up as in the front kick.

3. Pivot on your standing foot as you continue extending your knee forward. Your head should not sway from side to side.

4. Snap out your leg as in the front kick.

5. Face your opponent in proper kicking distance.

6. Quickly drive your knee up and begin turning as you pivot. Snap out to opponents mid-section.

6a. Kicking area is the top of the foot.

5

3

4

6

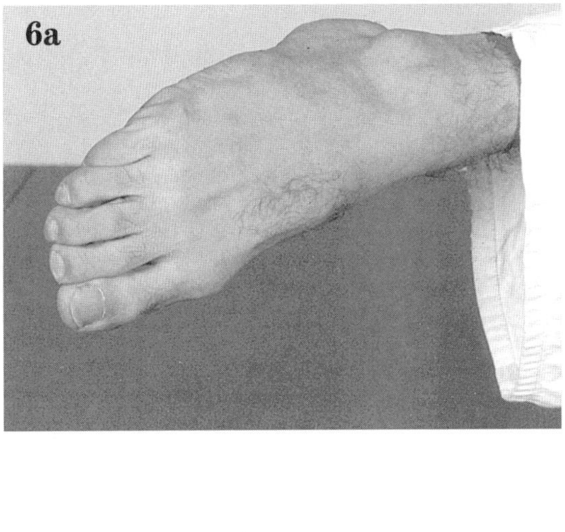

6a

This kick is fast and effective to all kicking zones.

7. You can sidekick high ...

8. midsection ...

9. or low...

7

8

9

Low roundhouse kick

1. Low roundhouse kick begins with a proper stance.

2. It is important to pivot even though you are not kicking high. Your knee does not lift very high.

3. Bend your standing leg slightly to allow you reach farther.

1

2

3

BASIC KICKS • INSIDE OUT ROUNDHOUSE KICK

Inside-out roundhouse kick

1. Inside-out roundhouse kick begins with a proper kicking stance.

2. Square your hips. Lift your knee up while placing your kicking foot in front of your standing leg.

3. Begin opening your knee to the side as you snap the kick out.

4

5

6

4. Face your opponent in a kicking stance.

5. Bring your right foot to kicking position.

6. Kick the attacker's mid-section

Back kick

1. To deliver a proper back kick you must be in a kicking stance.

2. Bring your knee up as you bend down. This is called a chambered up position. Prepare your foot for striking by pulling back your toes.

3. To enable full extension, bend your body down during the thrust of your kick. Your hips remain square to the ground. You can tell by how your toes keep pointing to the ground during the kick.

1

2

3

4. An attacker grabs you from behind. Assume a kicking stance.

5. Turn your head to face your attacker. Tuck your knee up to your body. Pull your toes back to kicking position.

6. Deliver a thrusting back kick to attacker's mid-section.

4

5

6

1

2

3

Back side kick

1. Stand in a kicking stance.

2. Back side kick begins with a pivot of your feet. You must turn your head over your shoulder so that you do not lose sight of your target.

3. Chamber up your leg as you did in back kick.

4. Extend out with a strong thrust as you bend your body down to counter balance your force.

4

5. You can deliver this kick when your attacker is in front of you. Face attacker with a kicking stance.

6. Pivot your front foot and turn your head to maintain eye contact with your attacker. Begin driving your hips towards the attacker to increase the momentum of your kick.

7. Chamber up your leg to ready your kick.

8. Thrust out your left heel to the attackerís mid-section.

Spin kick

1. Stand in your kicking stance

2. Pivot on your front foot and turn your head quickly in the same direction.

3. Bring your leg in high and wide of your target from the momentum generated from your spin.

4. To accelerate the kick through the target, extend and snap back your knee.

5

5. You can deliver this kick when your attacker is in front of you. Face attacker with a kicking stance.
6. Initiate your spin with a pivot of your front foot. Turn your head quickly to maintain eye contact with the attacker.
7. Extend your right leg and contact the attacker with your heel.
8. Continue following through to your initial kicking stance.

6

7

8

Sit down spin kick.

1. Ready kicking stance.

2. Turn your body and your head as you drop down to your left knee. Both your hands are placed on the ground.

3. Extend your leg as you maintain the momentum of your spin. Follow through the target area to complete the kick.

BASIC KICKS • SIT DOWN SPIN KICK

4. Face your attacker in a kicking stance.

5. Turn and drop to one knee. Touch both hands on the ground.

6. Extend your left leg as you continue to spin.

7. Your kick is to the back of attacker's knee.

Sit down roundhouse kick

1. Ready kicking stance.

2. Drop to your front knee and touch both hands on the ground.

3. Pick up your left knee in a chambered up position.

4. Snap out your roundhouse kick.

5. Face your attacker in a kicking stance.

6. Pivot on your front foot and begin to deliver chambered kicking leg towards attacker's knee.

7. Ensure your hands are on the ground to deliver maximum power on your roundhouse kick.

Master Choe

BASIC STEPS

Training in the martial arts is exciting and comes in may varieties to maintain anyone's interest. Kicking targets is one of the many drills in the martial arts. It can be practiced individually, or in the discipline of a group.

Hap Ki Do is an open hand martial art that involves pins, arm locks, throws and choke holds. These are done safely and with respect for your opponent.

STEP FORWARD

Stance and focus are the basic of delivering effective technique. Your stance will give to you balance to deliver power. Focus will concentrate your motion, thought, and reactive abilities. You should center your sight and allow peripheral vision to see everything around that central stare.

1. Fighting stance will give you the ability to react in a variety of ways. Your back foot is turned sideways for stability. Your front foot is facing in front allowing your body to face in front. Left hand will be open and out at your chest level. This hand will primarily provide blocking and initial grabbing ability. Your right hand will be open and about a hand width beside your left elbow. Make sure your back is straight and your chin is down.

2. Advancing with your right leg will bring your right hand over your left hand and in the now forward position. Feet and hands have now switched position from before.

1

2

DEEP STEP

1. Attacker grabs your left wrist with his right hand.
2. Front stance will be a powerful reaction to initiate your technique. Your left leg will step long and wide bending deeply at the knee. Back leg will support forward motion by almost locking straight and digging back foot into the ground. Back remains straight. Simultaneously raise your left hand as you step. This will weaken attacker's grip by his hand to an awkward holding position towards his own shoulder. Bring your right hand across to your left elbow to block your body region.

1

2

HALF-TURN STEP

1. Half turn step will begin to give you circular leverage. Face forward in fighting stance ready position.

2. Pivoting clockwise on your left foot.

3. Finish your step in a fighting stance. You will now be facing where you came from.

PRACTICAL APPLICATION

1. Attacker grabs your right wrist with his left hand.

2. Pivot counter-clockwise on your right foot. Place your left leg behind him before your body has completely turned.

3. Finish turning your body to achieve your fighting stance. This will bring attacker's hold to weak and awkward position giving you superiority.

FULL-TURN STEP

1. Forward turn step starts with your left leg in front.

2. Pivot counter-clockwise on your left foot as you step forward. Right arm straightens out and forward. Left hand comes to your right shoulder.

3. Finish fighting stance on opposite side. Face where you came from.

PRACTICAL APPLICATION

1. Attacker garbs your left wrist with his left hand.

2. Use your right arm as a fulcrum by pushing his left hand in opposite direction hyper extending attacker's elbow.

3. Pivot counter-clockwise on your left foot as you step forward. Place your right arm just behind his left elbow.

1

2

3

TURNING STEP

1. Turning step will allow you to face attacker that is behind you. Attacker grabs your right wrist with his right hand behind you.

2. Pivot on both your feet, turn clockwise to face the attacker while raising your right hand in a circular motion to the ready position. This motion will place your right hand over the attacker's right wrist giving you a leverage position. Your left hand comes across to your right elbow to block your body.

SELF-DEFENSE

1

Technique 1

1. Attacker grabs your lapel with his right hand (thumb down). ***Son-Mok-Kuk-Gi***

2. Grab his right wrist (fingers over) with your left hand. Grab his right hand (fingers over) with your right hand.

3. Step strongly into attacker with your left foot. Create a bend on attacker's right wrist by pulling his arm in with your left hand. Immediately turn his right fingers skyward causing stress on attacker's wrist.

2

3

4. Turn your body to your right pulling attacker's right arm across your chest.

5. Lean over onto attacker's right elbow.

Technique 2

1. Attacker grabs you by the lapel with his right hand. ***Son-Mok-kuk-Gi***

2. Reach over his hand with your right hand. Turn his hand over by turning your body and pulling him slightly towards you. That will assist your hand strength. Place your left arm on his elbow locking it straight.

3. In the circular motion by stepping through with your left foot. Begin applying pressure on his elbow with your left hand and by leaning your weight on it as he is forced to the ground.

4. Right foot has take a small step. On the ground, push on his back of hand with your grabbing hand towards his shoulder.

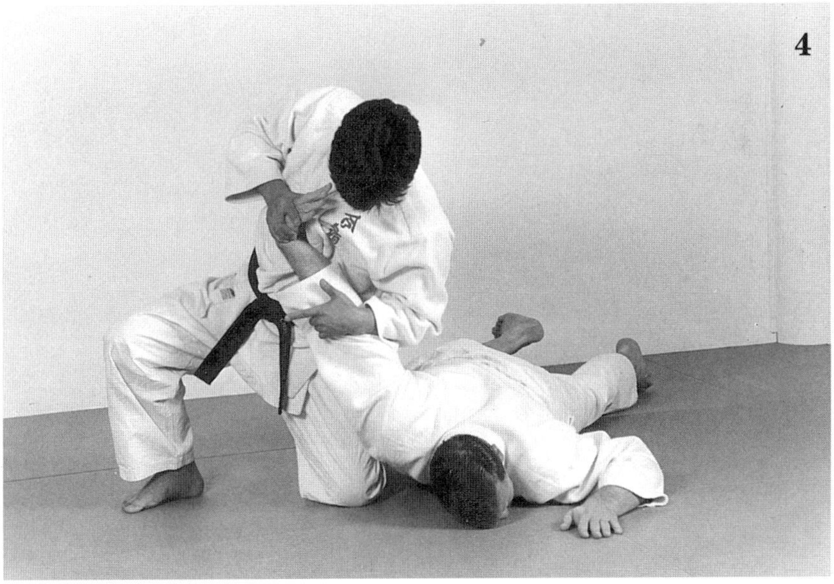

Technique 3

1. The attacker grabs you by the belt in an attempt to unbalance your center of gravity. ***Son-Mok-kuk-Gi***

2. Place your right hand with your thumb on top directly on his. Place left hand (fingers over) directly on his wrist.

3. Turn your hips and extend his arm out to give you a superior position. Making sure his wrist is straight push down on his wrist with your left hand and assist the pressure on his wrist with your right hand, His grab on your belt will contribute to making a wrist lock.

4. The pain will drop him to the ground. Continue applying pressure. Pin him down by dropping your left knee on his shoulder.

1

Technique 4

1. The attacker grabs your clothes at the left elbow with his right hand. ***Son-Mok-kuk-Gi***

2. Place your right hand(fingers over) on his and grab firmly. Make a circle around the outside of his arm with your left arm.

2

3. As you come over his arm, begin applying pressure straight down his wrist join area with your arm. Maintain a firm hold on his hand and turn his wrist up. This will cause a sharp pain in wrist bringing the attacker to the ground.

4. Lean forward as the attacker goes down to maintain pressure.

5. The insert shows how the wrist remains straight with the attacker's forearm causing pressure only to the joint in one direction. It helps to keep his grab with your right hand. Also notice how you never bend down rather lean forward over the wrist keeping pressure and gaining strength throughout the technique.

Technique 5

1. The attacker grabs your right wrist with both of his hands. ***Son-Mok-Kuk-Gi***

2. Bring your hand up in a circular motion inside out until it is in front of your forehead. Place your left hand (fingers over) on attackers right fingers.

3

3. Hold attacker's hand in place as you drive your hand down on the attacker's wrist with fingers open wide.

4. You form a wrist lock by holding the attacker's hand in place. He can pull his hand away unless you press firmly forward with your right hand taking his strength away. The technique is delivered nice and straight without any turning of your body or swinging of your arms.

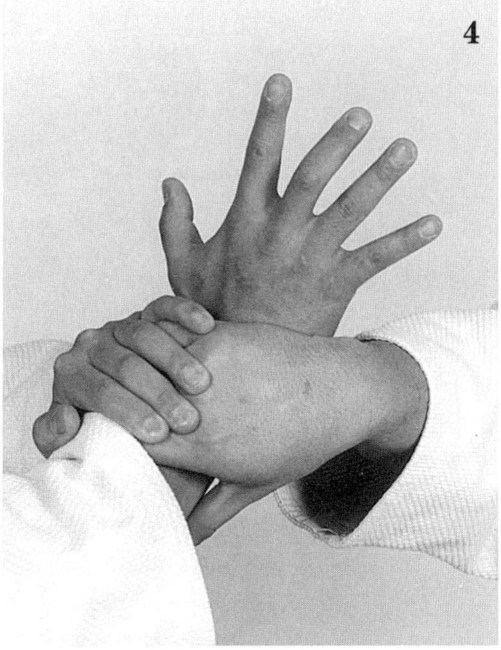
4

1

Technique 6

1. The attacker grabs both your wrists with both of his hands.

2. In a circular motion bring your left hand (fingers over) the outside of attacker's right wrist. At the same time, grab attacker's right hand with your right hand. Before grabbing attacker's right wrist with your left hand, force attacker's right wrist to bend against the area between your left index finger and thumb.

2

3. Proceed to grabbing attacker's right wrist with left hand. Ensure elbow is bent before applying a downward and over force on the attacker's wrist. Lean forward by transferring weight to your left leg as you step with it towards attacker. This will maintain maximum control.

1

2

3

Technique 7

1. The attacker grabs your left wrist with his right hand.
   Pal-Kum-Chi

2. Place your right hand (fingers over) on his. Make a circular motion with your left arm to the outside of his right arm. Release his hold by bending his wrist with your right hand and pushing through his thumb with your left hand.

3. Maintain the bend in his wrist as you grab his right elbow with your left hand. Apply pressure to hyper extend his elbow. Keep the right hand in front and close to you.

4. This will drop the attacker heavily to the ground.

5. Pin him with your left knee and continue the pressure on elbow and wrist.

1

Technique 8

1. The attacker grabs both your wrists with both of his hands. ***Pal-Kum-Chi***

2. With a circular motion bring the left hand to the outside allowing you to grab his right wrist (fingers over) with the same left hand. Your right hand grabs his right hand (fingers over) at the same time.

3. Place your left hand on his right elbow to apply pressure. Continue in the circular motion by stepping through with the left foot.

2

3

4. Right foot has taken a small step by the time the attacker has hit the ground. Place your left knee on the ground for stability while ensuring that the attacker's arm is in a vertical position. Pressure on his wrist and elbow is being applied for control.

5. Using your right hand, place attacker's arm against your left shoulder. His right palm will point out, With your left forearm maintain pressure on elbow by squeezing his elbow to your body.

6. Increase pressure by bringing your right forearm on his right triceps and squeezing to your body.

4

5

6

Technique 9

1. The attacker grabs your right wrist with both of his hands. ***Pal-Kum-Chi***

2. Lean forward while straightening your arm towards a point high above his right shoulder.

3. Draw your arm across towards his left shoulder. This will allow you to grab his right wrist (fingers over) with your right hand. Place left hand on his right elbow. The draw is continually bringing the attacker's right hand closer to you keeping his right elbow straight and out in front of him. Apply pressure on his elbow with your left hand.

4. The pressure on his elbow will keep him off balance and quickly bring him down at your feet. Pressure is maintained once on the ground. Ensure your superior position by al ways keeping his right shoulder below the level of his right hand.

Technique 10

1. Attacker grabs your left wrist with his right hand.
   Pal-kum-chi

2. Place your right hand(fingers over) on his right hand while making a circular motion inside out with your left hand. This will allow you to grab his right wrist (fingers over) with your left hand.

3

3. Swing your left elbow over his right elbow. Immediately lean tilting his arm to a vertical position. When the attacker's arm is in a vertical position, you can maintain pressure on his elbow by squeezing towards your body. Also apply pressure on attacker's wrist by pushing his right palm towards his right shoulder.

4

4. Continue leaning until the attacker and your left knee is on the ground. You can maintain pressure for control of the attacker.

5

Technique 11

1. Attacker grabs your right wrist with his right hand. *Boo-Chae*

2. Place your left hand (fingers over-thumb down) on attacker's right thumb. Your fingers will be on the palm and your thumb on the back of the hand. In a circular motion bring your right hand up and over bending your right elbow. This will allow you to leverage out of attacker's grip.

3. Immediately grab attacker's right hand to double the grip you al ready have with your left hand. This is called a scissors hold.

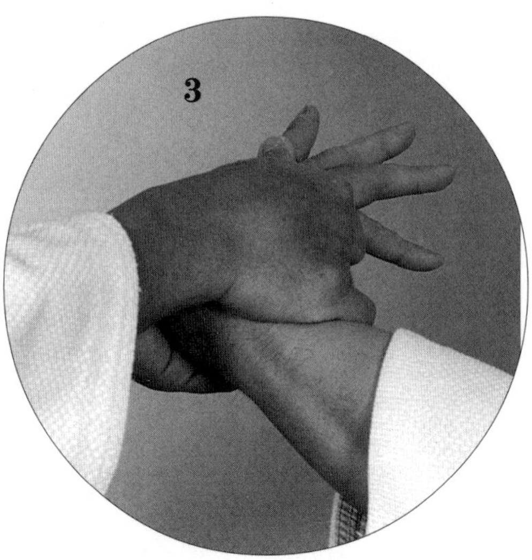

4. Maintain a 90° bend on attacker's right wrist and elbow to maximize leverage. Step back with left leg so that you are standing facing the same way as attacker. Your feet now match his. Throughout the step, you are pushing the attacker's wrist over. His palm faces the ground.

5. When attacker is down, pin him by extending his arm (palm to the ground) and press your right knee against his elbow. You can increase pressure by pulling his hand upwards in opposite direction.

1

Technique 12

1. Attacker grabs your right wrist with both his hands.
   Boo-Chae

2. Tilt your right hand up so it passes between and above his arms. Your leverage is achieved by bending your elbow. Grab around his right thumb with your left hand. Continue to bend your right elbow to release his left hand grip.

2

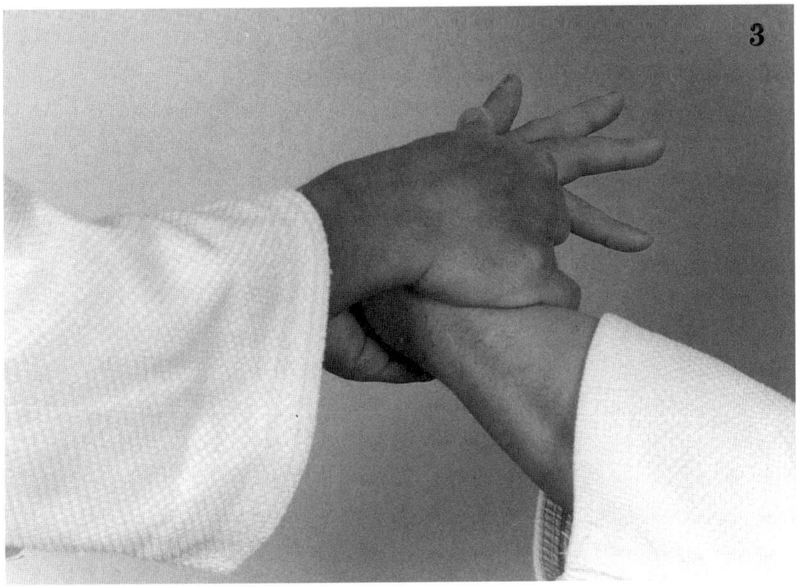
3

3. Focus on his right hand. Obtain a scissors hold with both your hands.

4. Step back with your left leg until facing the same direction as your attacker. Without stopping your turning motion, you would have been pressing down and over on his wrist throughout the step.

4

Technique 13

1. Attacker grabs both your wrists. ***Boo-Chae***

2. Turn both your palms towards you in a double inside turn. Make sure your left hand is on top facing you while the other slips under attacker's right hand. Grab, palm upwards, the back of attacker's right hand and around his thumb with your right hand. Continuing the small circle will release your left hand from attacker's grip.

3. Place your left hand on the back of attacker's right hand achieving a scissors hold.

4. Notice how the pressure is in a linear direction. Once the proper angle is achieved, you can double your grip to apply maximum linear pressure.

5. You may now apply pressure on attacker's wrist while stepping back with your left leg. Once the attacker is on the ground, achieve a pin. This is done by extending his arm (palm facing the ground) and dropping your right knee against his elbow.

3

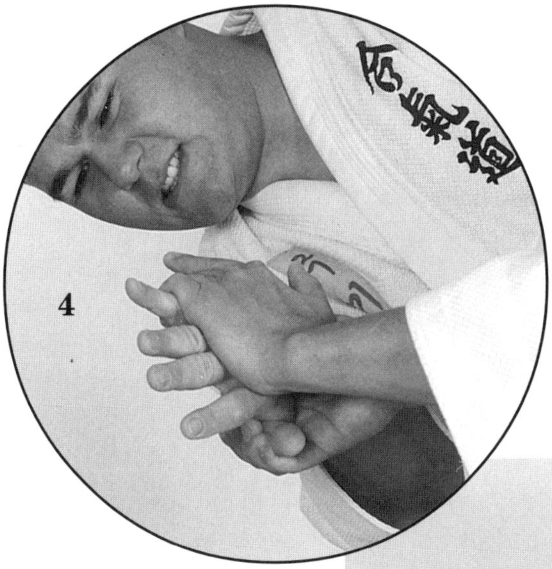
4

5

Technique 14

1. Attacker grabs your right wrist with his right hand. ***Hei-Jun***

2. Place your left hand(thumbs up) on the back of his right hand. Advance your right leg while swinging his right hand high in front of you.

3. Continue this motion with an advance of your left leg. You feet will now match his.

4. Pivot 180° on the ball of both of your feet to face the direction you came from. As you pivot, bring his hand directly over your head until you have it over his right shoulder. With your scissors hold established at the beginning bend his wrist towards you.

4a. Continue this motion as if striking down with a sword in your hands.

5. Without having stopped your motion, continue bringing his hand over his shoulder and down to the ground. Pressure is maintained on the wrist by pulling the hand towards your body.

6. On the ground execute a pin by releasing your left hand and placing it on his right elbow. Press down on the elbow and pull on the hand until the attacker's elbow touches the ground.

6

5

4

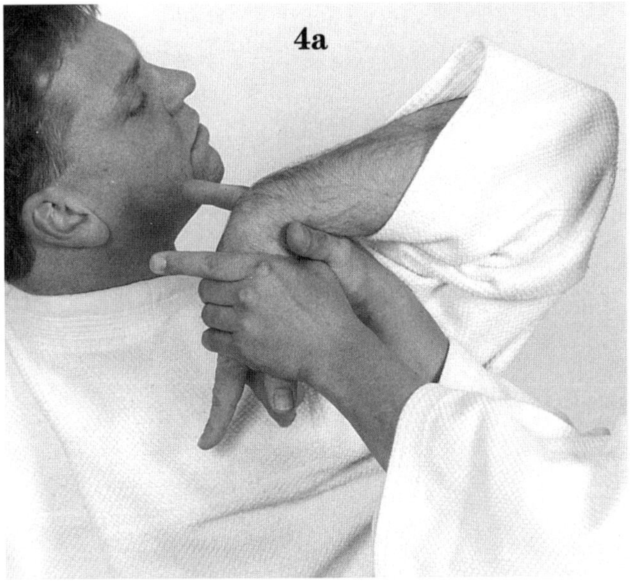
4a

Technique 15

1. Attacker grabs both your hands with both of his hands. ***Hei-Jun***

2. Place your right hand on his right wrist. Push his right hand in front of you by advancing with your right leg. Keep your body low so that his hands are at your shoulder level.

3. Advance with your left foot to match his stance.

4. Turn around quickly. Slide your hand from his right wrist to his right hand. This will enable you to pull his hand towards your body putting pressure on his wrist.

5. Continue your motion bringing attacker's right hand over his shoulder and down to the ground. Pin him by pushing his elbow to the ground with your left hand.

Technique 16

1. Attacker grabs your right wrist with both his hands. ***Hei-Jun***

2. Grab attacker's wrist with your left hand. Push his hand forward in a circular motion with a strong step of your right foot.

3. Step through with your left foot bringing attacker hand high in front of your forehead. Establish a scissors hold on attacker's right hand.

4. Pivot 180° clockwise eventually bringing attacker's hand over his shoulder. Follow through to the ground.

4

3

Technique 17

1. Attacker grabs your left wrist with his right hand.
   Hei-Jun

2. Grab attacker's wrist with your left hand. Push his hand forward in a circular motion with a strong step of your right foot.

3

3. Step through with your left foot bringing attacker's hand high in front of your forehead. Establish a scissors hold on attacker's right hand.

4. Continue the motion to the ground.

4

Technique 18

1. Attacker grabs your left wrist with his right hand. ***Yuk-Hei-Jun***

2. Grab attacker's inside right wrist with your right hand. Lift hand to attacker's shoulder level. Step behind attacker with your right foot pivoting clockwise on your left foot.

3. Now pivot on both feet continuing the clockwise turn. Bring the attacker's hand directly over your head (Do not raise too high because of his body turning).

4. Continue motion down and over his right shoulder. Apply pressure throughout by bending the attacker's wrist towards you with your right hand. Support this motion with your left hand.

4

3

1

Technique 19

1. Attacker grabs your right wrist with his right hand. ***Yun-Hang***

2. Place your left hand on the back of attacker's right wrist. Step forward with your left leg and in a circular motion bring attacker's hand up.

3. Continue the circular motion by stepping forward with your right leg and pivoting counter-clockwise. Through the pivot, the attacker's hand is brought over your head. There will be great pressure applied on attacker's wrist by pulling his right back hand towards his right elbow.

2

3

4. Continue turning in the same direction bring your right leg to the right side of his body. Straighten his arm by applying pressure downward on his elbow until it is parallel to the ground.

5. Continued pressure will bring the attacker to the ground. Pin his elbow down with your right hand and apply pressure on his wrist by bending it upwards with your left hand.

1

2

Technique 20

1. Attacker grabs your right wrist with both his hands. ***Yun-Hang***

2. Place your left hand on the back of attacker's hand. Step forward with your left leg and in a circular motion bring attacker's hand across and up.

3. With a double grip twist his hand horizontally until his palm faces the ground.

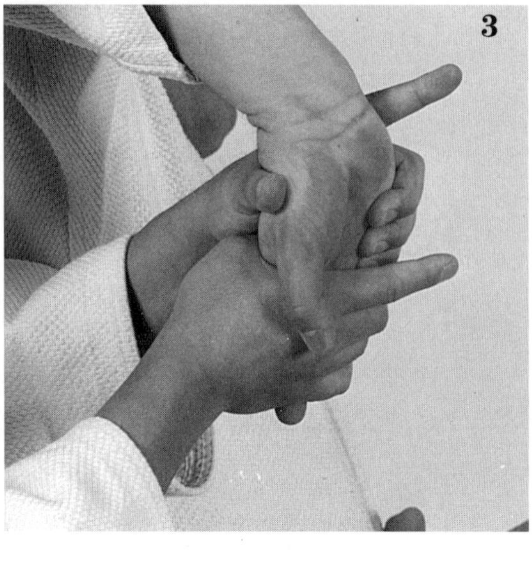

3

4

5

4. Left leg steps forward allowing you to turn into the attacker. Place left hand on his elbow and bend his four fingers back.

5. Continue to turn your body by pivoting on both your feet. Bring attacker's fingers over his shoulder keeping the elbow bent for leverage.

6. Continue the motion to the ground. Pull up the attacker's fingers up towards you.

7. A close up shows how by grabbing your right wrist with your left hand locks his hand and gives you maximum leverage.

6

7

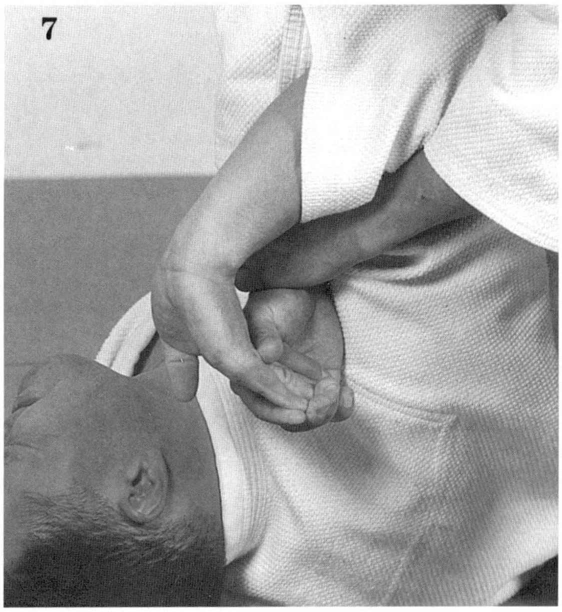

Technique 21

1. Attacker grabs your left clothing at the elbow with his right hand. ***Yun-Hang***

2. Grab attacker's inside right wrist with your right hand. In a circular motion lift your left arm under attacker's right hand.

3. Step forward with your right leg so you are behind attacker. As you step, pivot counter-clockwise bringing attacker's right hand under his same arm towards his armpit. Apply pressure by lifting your left arm and twisting his right wrist with your right hand.

4. Step backward with your left leg while re-adjusting arm hold. Release pressure and bend attacker's right wrist in opposite direction with right hand. Facilitate the wrist bend by placing attacker's right elbow against your right elbow with your left hand.

5. Having attained control pivot quickly counter-clockwise bringing attacker's hand over his right shoulder.

6. Continue the motion to the ground with a small left step backwards. Place left knee on the ground and pin.

6

5

4

Technique 22

1. Attacker grabs your left wrist with his right hand.
   Yun-Hang

2. Pivot counter-clockwise as you step in 180° leading with your right leg followed by your left leg. Bring attacker's hand over your head while stepping. Pressure is applied by lifting of attacker's fingers with your left back hand and pulling down in opposite direction with your right hand.

3. The pressure will release your left hand from attacker's grip and allow you to place it on attacker's right elbow.

4. Pivot counter-clockwise putting attacker's right elbow against your right elbow. As you pivot bring attacker's hand behind his right shoulder.

5. Drop him to the ground and pin with your left hand by pressing his elbow down.

6

4

3

Master Choe 2 person self defense

THROWING TECHNIQUES

Technique 1

1. Attacker grabs your clothes at the left elbow with his right hand.
2. Grab his clothes the same way with your left hand.
3. Step on the inside of his right foot with your right foot. Hook your right arm around attacker's neck so that his head is close to your right shoulder.
4. Step on the inside of attacker's right foot with your left foot. Bend forward so that he begins to wrap around your body. You must touch your left hip on his center of gravity. This will make him light to throw. Ensure your feet are turned a little outward. This will allow your knees to bend outwards.

3

4

5. Continue to bend and pull around your body.
6. Your right hand follows through to your left knee. Your left hand follows through to your left hip as you lift the attacker with your legs. Make sure not to lift until attacker's weight has transferred onto you.
7. Attacker will travel over you and land at your feet. Maintain your hold by going down on your right knee.
8. Choke by dropping your right shoulder on attacker's neck. Tighten your right arm around his neck to finish the choke. Ensure that your right thumb is pointing towards you.

7

8

1

Technique 2

1. Attacker grabs your clothes at the left elbow with his right hand.

2. Grab attacker's right arm with your left hand to mirror his grab.

3. Step on the inside of his right foot with your right foot. Hook under your arm under attacker's right shoulder.

2

3

4. Step on the inside of attacker's left foot with your left foot. Bend forward so that he begins to wrap around your body.

5. Your right hand follows through to your left knee. Your left hand follows through to your left hip as you lift the attacker with your legs. Make sure not to lift until attacker's weight has transferred onto you.

6. Continue the motion until the attacker is completely on your back. Your head is up and looking where the attacker is going to fall.

6

5

4

1

Technique 3

1. Attacker is facing you in a closed stance. You both have your right legs back.

2. Attack is a right step, right hand punch. Block with your left forearm. Immediately grab the clothes with your left hand. Transfer your weight forward to support your block.

3. Step forward between attacker's feet with your right foot. Pull attacker's right arm over your shoulder to place his torso across the back of your neck. Your right arm hooks around the back of his right thigh. Pull his center of gravity on your shoulder.

4. You are now able to lift attacker with his weight spread evenly across your shoulders.

2

3

4

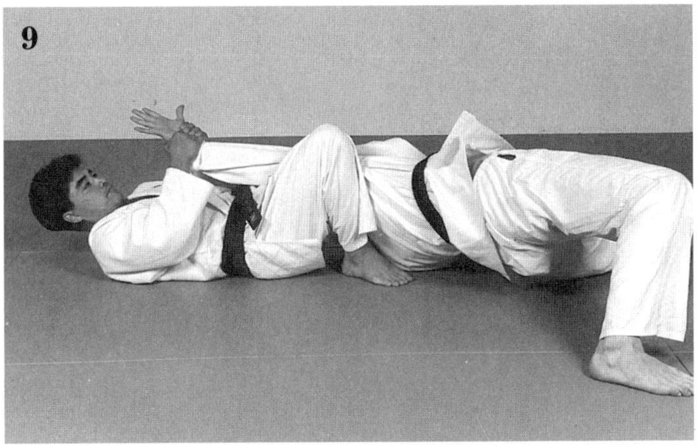

5. Tilt your shoulders-right up and left down-quickly. You are not lifting his body weight rather transferring it over you. Continue to pull left arm across the front of your body as you release attacker's right leg.

6. Attacker will fall heavily to the ground by your leg.

7. Step your right shin into attacker's ribs as you grab a good hold of attacker's right hand with both your hands. Ensure his palm is pointing away from you.

8. Step over attacker's neck with your left foot as you sit down and fall back. Make sure you are perpendicular to the attacker.

9. Squeeze the attacker's arm between your knees and apply pressure by lifting your hips.

1

2

3

Technique 4

1. You are locked in a throwing grab with your opponent.

2. You will have to break opponent's balance to gain an advantage. Step between the attacker's feet with your right foot. At the same time, pull his right shoulder towards you and push his left shoulder away from you. The opponent's balance should be broken.

3. Quickly change the direction of the turn as opponent tries to regain his balance. Pull attacker's left shoulder down and push his right shoulder over his left.

4. This turn will place your left hand in easy access to his right leg. Release your left hold to grab opponent's right ankle. Don't grab just hook your hand. Your right hand is high on opponent's shoulder. The circular motion you started no grows larger as your hands are farther apart. Your center of gravity is lower than your opponent. These points are the basics of successful Dun-Ji-Gi.

5. With a larger circular motion, pull opponent's ankle to your waist and push his shoulder over. Opponent will not be able to resist falling.

6. Place your right knee on the inside of opponent's left thigh to pin. Continue to hold his right leg under your left arm. Lean your body weight forward onto your right thumb that is placed on opponent's throat.

4

5

6

1

2

Technique 5

1. The attacker is facing you with a closed stance. He steps with his right leg to deliver a right punch.

2. Step forward with your left leg and block with your left forearm. While your block is there, grab the attacker's clothes with your left hand.

3. Step on the inside of his right foot with your right foot. Hook your right arm under attacker's right shoulder.

4. Step on the inside of attacker's left foot with your left foot. Bend forward sot that he begins to wrap around your body.

5. Your right hand goes to your left knee. Your left hand goes to your left hip. Continue the motion until the attacker is completely on your back. Your head is up and looking where the attacker is going to fall.

6. Pop your legs straight to project the attacker over your back and continue to turn.

7. Once at your feet, prepare to finish.

3

4

7

8

6

9

5

8. Wrap your left arm around his elbow so that it is tucked under your arm. Place your right hand on attacker's shoulder joint. Reach your left hand to your right wrist and grab. Place attacker's right arm against your left thigh. Lock attacker's body with your right knee.

9. Apply pressure by leaning back on attacker's right forearm with your upper body. The arm lock will not allow the attacker's upper arm to move putting all the pressure on his right elbow. Make sure that the attacker's elbow is slightly bent with his thumb pointing to the ground.

1

2

3

Technique 6

1. You are locked in a throwing grab with your opponent.

2. Sit down and fall to your back without releasing your hold. His head will be driven to the ground. Continue to throw him over your body by placing your right foot in the inside of his left thigh.

3. As you go on your back, lift up and over without releasing your hold.

4. Keep yourself close to him during the throw. Kick over with your right leg to finish the throw.

5. Pull yourself over and on top of the attacker.

6. Finish with a choke-hold. Straddle your legs on attacker. Place left hand on the ground to lift your body high while pulling your right forearm to your right shoulder. As you lift your body, the attacker's head will bend forward against your forearm causing a choke. The choke will be most effective if your right palm faces your chest.

4

5

6

Technique 7

1. Attacker grabs your shoulders with both his hands.

2. Slide your right hand (palm up) under his right collar. Grab the clothes with your thumb in the outside. Left hand grabs the clothes under attacker's right elbow.

3. Place your right shin parallel to the ground across attacker's waist. The top of your right foot is at the attacker's right side.

4. Swing your left leg over attacker's right arm by dropping your body down at his feet. You will fall lightly by hanging on to him as you go down. You will land on your back.

5. Your left calf is now placed against attacker's left jaw.

6. This left leg will aid in pushing the attacker over.

Continued on next page.

4

5

6

Continued from previous page.

7. The pulling of your grab against your leg force will place leg attacker's chin in the pocket behind your knee. This can create tremendous pressure.

8. The attacker will be able to resist the throw as he falls over your body.

9. The initial grabbing was all planned for this final position. The attacker has fallen into your arm lock. You can also maintain the initial pressure on his neck and head with your hold.

THROWING DEFENSE

Technique 1

1. Attacker engages you in a throwing hold. Right hand on the lapel and left hand on the elbow clothing.

2. Block attacker's throwing attempt by stepping forward with your left leg and pushing with your left hand against his lower back. You must do this before he can gain a leverage position.

3. Slide your arm over his head. Push his head back by placing your elbow under his chin as you step wider with your left leg.

4. Bring attacker down across your left knee as you go down on your right knee. Apply a choke by pulling his lapel towards you as you push his head back with your left arm.

4

3

Technique 2

1. Attacker engages you in a throwing hold. Right hand on the lapel and left hand on the elbow clothing.

2. Your attacker attempts a throw. Counter by stepping back with your left foot and grabbing your opponent's right hand with your left hand.

3. Quickly pivot transferring your weight across to your left foot. Push down attacker's throat with your right thumb. Keep your weight over this pressure you are applying.

4. Slide your right knee forward and on top of opponent's right shoulder. Double your hold on attacker's right hand and continue turning his wrist to the outside. It is important to maintain pressure on his wrist throughout the technique because it is a good control mechanism.

4

3

1

Technique 3

1. Attacker engages you in a throwing hold. Right hand on the lapel and left hand on the elbow clothing.

2. Block attacker's throwing attempt by stepping forward with your left leg and pushing with your left hand against his lower back. You must do this before he can gain a leverage position.

2

3. Arc your opponent backwards by pushing on his lower back and pulling his head towards you. You must make this technique continuous for best results. Make sure his chin is tucked on top of your elbow.

4. Drop down to your right knee bringing him down with you. Clasps your hands together and apply a choke by squeezing his neck close to your body. You want to pull his neck towards you while pushing his head in the other direction with your shoulder. That will cause the head to tilt against the choke maximizing the results.

4

3

Technique 4

1. Attacker engages you in a throwing hold. Right hand on the lapel and left hand on the elbow clothing.

2. The attacker lunges to your front leg in an attempt to take you down. Release your right hand hold and bring it up under his left arm.

3. Bring your right weight forward tucking his head under your arm. Distribute your weight over his shoulders. Your right hand comes closer to your right shoulder closing the hold on his arm.

6

7

5

8

4

4. Your left hand reaches across his back and grabs his belt. Your right hand grabs the clothing.

5. Drop to your seat as you pull him up. Assist the throw by lifting with your right leg on the inside of attacker's left leg.

6. The momentum from doing this quickly will toss the attacker completely over you.

7. He will land on the ground over you.

8. Lock his right arm in between your legs. Clasp your hands together and squeeze his neck towards you to apply a choke.

Technique 5

1. You are in a throwing hold with your opponent.

2. The attacker lunges for your front leg in an attempt to take you down. Release your right grab and bring your right hand under his armpit. Transfer your weight to the right leg.

4

3

3. With your weight on your right leg, you will allow your left leg to come around in a counter-clockwise turn. Drop down to your left knee as you clasp your hands together around the attacker's left shoulder. Dropping down to your knee will keep attacker from lifting up to regain balance. Therefore maintain downward pressure over his shoulder.

4. Continue to bring attacker down until you are completely over him and he is pressed to the ground. With nowhere left to go, continued pressure attacks the shoulder joint.

1

Technique 6

1. You and your attacker are in a throwing hold.

2. The attacker lunges to your right leg allow you right leg to come back with him as you T-bar him placing your weight on his back. Your weight hold was released to bring under his left arm and bring over his back.

3. Slide your left leg under him and pull his body into you as you go to the ground.

4. Tuck attacker's head under your right knee and lock your feet together. Lie back bringing the attacker's left arm with you.

5. Squeeze your legs and straighten your body. Pull his left hand down with your right hand. Slide your left hand through the triangle you have just made until you can grab your right wrist. Apply pressure on his wrist and choke him with your legs.

2

5

4

3

OFFENSE TECNIQUES

OFFENSE TECHNIQUES

Technique 1

1. You are facing attacker in a closed stance. Both have right foot back. ***Pal-Kum-Chi***

2. Step forward with your right foot making sure it travels behind your left foot. Your legs will be crossed over. You will be close enough to grab attacker's left wrist with your left hand.

3. Deliver a left leg side-kick to the attacker's left side.

4. Place your left foot down beside attacker's left foot then step forward with your right. Meanwhile, place your right hand against attacker's left elbow. Apply pressure as you pivot counter-clockwise.

5. Add another left foot step to the pivot increasing the circular momentum.

6. The attacker will fall down at your feet by pulling him towards you as he falls. Pin by placing your right knee down heavily on the attacker's right shoulder and continuing the pressure on his left elbow.

6

5

4

Technique 2

1. You are facing attacker in a closed stance. Both have right foot back. ***Yun-Hang***

2. Grab attacker's front hand with your left hand. Raise it to expose his ribs where you deliver a right hand punch. Make sure you step forward with your right foot to get the proper striking distance.

3. Pivot counter-clockwise on your right foot to get behind attacker's left arm. Grab attacker's left elbow with your right hand.

4. Apply downward pressure on his elbow to bring his body down.

5. This will force the attacker to the ground and you can pin by placing your right knee down on his left shoulder.

5

4

1

Technique 3

1. You are facing the attacker in an open stance. ***Hei-Jun***

2. Step forward and to the side with your right foot achieving a horse riding stance. At the same time, grab attacker's right wrist with your left hand. Strike the attacker's right side with your right fist.

3. Scoop the attacker's right hand down then high in front of you. During this circular motion achieve a scissors hold.

2

3

4. Step with your left foot forward then pivot clockwise on both feet bringing attacker's hand directly over your head. Continue your motion behind attacker's right shoulder.

5. The attacker will be forced to the ground at your feet.

6. Extend attacker's arm straight and holding the hand high, press down on his elbow with your right knee.

6

5

4

Technique 4

1. To arrest an individual, approach him form behind. ***Hei-Jun***

2. Go to his right with your right step. Grab his right wrist in a scissors hold with both your hands.

3. Step again with your left foot. Raise attacker's hand high in front of you.

4. Pivot clockwise on both feet bringing his hand over your head.

5. Your scissors hold will rotate his arm counter-clockwise putting pressure on his wrist and shoulder.

6. Following through on this motion will bring the attacker to the ground.

6

5

4

Technique 5

1. Arresting the individual from behind right side. ***Son-Mok-Kuk-Gi***

2. Step with the right foot when in grabbing distance. Grab his right wrist with your right hand. Place your left hand under his arm with your thumb pointing skyward.

3. Step in with your left leg. Hook your left elbow around his right elbow. Bring his right arm up with your right hand. Achieve a greater bend in his wrist the higher you bring it up. Pull his right hand towards his elbow(your chest) to apply pressure on his wrist.

4. Step forward with your right foot and pivot counter-clockwise on both feet. While doing so, push his right elbow across your body and against your right forearm with your left hand. Push his right wrist over his right shoulder.

5. This motion will bring him to the ground. His elbow must point skyward. This will give you maximum leverage when pulling upward on his hand.

6. Press his elbow to the ground while pulling on his right hand.

Technique 6

1. Approach individual from behind. ***Mok-Jo-Ru-Gi***

2. Step your right foot in between his feet. Place your left hand on his right shoulder.

3. Reach around his neck with your right arm. Clasp your hands together with your left palm up and your right palm down.

4. Step back with your left foot pulling him backwards to the ground.

5. Go down on your left knee introducing your right knee to his spine while continuing to apply choke.

Technique 7

1. Approach individual from behind. ***Mok-Jo-Ru-Gi***

2. Step your right foot in between his feet. Reach your left hand under his with your thumb pointing up. Hold his right shoulder with your right hand.

3. Your left arm raises his left arm high and back. Your right arm reaches around his neck grabbing his left collar as high as possible. Ensure that your thumb is on the skin side of his clothes.

4. To apply the choke push your left hand against the back of his head while pulling his clothes tight across his neck.

5. Step back with your left foot pulling him backwards and down.

6. Go down on your left knee.

7. Open your right knee to the side and pull him across your inside thigh. This will bring his body weight onto the choke increasing the pressure.

Master Choe jumping back side kick

WEAPONS SELF-DEFENSE

Knife defense.

1. Attacker has a knife in his right hand. You are both standing in an open stance. Your right leg is back. Attacker's left leg is back. ***Hei-Jun***

2. Attacker thrust at you with right leg and knife. Step back with your left foot and deflect his thrust downward with a scissors hold.

3. Step forward and to the right with your left foot bringing the knife high and in front of you.

4. Pivot clockwise on both feet bringing the knife directly over your head. Continue the motion over attacker's right shoulder and to the ground.

1

2

Sword defense

1. Attacker has a sword with his right leg forward. You are standing with your right leg back. ***Boo-Chae***

2. Attacker strikes downward while advancing with his right foot. Transfer your weight to your left leg and out of the way of the strike. Ensure avoiding the strike by parrying the attacker's right hand away with your left hand.

3. Obtain a scissor hold on attacker's right hand. Twisting your body to your left, turn the attacker's wrist over.

4. Continue this motion by stepping in the same direction with your right foot. Follow through until the attacker is on the ground.

3

4

Gun defense

1. Attacker has a gun against your forehead. The gun is in his right hand. ***Hei-Jun***

2. Step forward and to the right with your right foot. At the same time, grab attacker's right wrist with your left hand. Punch attacker's right ribs with your right hand.

3. In a circular motion, swing attacker's hand low in front of you then up to your eye level. Obtain a scissor hold on attacker's right hand.

4. Step forward with your left foot continuing the circular motion high.

5. Pivot clockwise on both feet bringing the gun above your head then over the attacker's right shoulder to the ground.

1

Long Stick defense
Technique 1

1. Attacker has a staff in his hands. You are both in an open stance. You have your right leg back. Attacker has his left leg back. ***Dun-Ji-Gi***

2. Attacker strikes down at you while advancing with his right leg. Step forward with you left foot. Grab the staff between his grip with your right hand. Grab the staff directly over your head with your left hand. Your grips have your thumbs pointing towards attacker.

3. Step behind attacker with your right foot. Turn the staff clockwise so that your left hand is high in front of you. Your right hand is beside your right temple.

2

3

4. Imagine striking down as your attacker did but in the direction you now face. This will drive attacker's hands behind his head and knock him off balance.

5. Once on the ground, step forward with your left foot and strike attacker.

5

4

Long Stick Defense Technique 2

1. Attacker has a staff in his hands. You are both in an open stance. You have your right leg back. Attacker has his left leg back. ***Pal-Kum-Chi & Boo-Chae***

2. Attacker thrusts towards you. Transfer your weight to your left leg and out of the way of the thrust. Ensure avoiding the thrust by parrying the attacker's right hand away with your left hand. Obtain a scissor hold on attacker's right hand.

3. Step clockwise with your right foot so that you are facing the same way as attacker.

4. Turn your body 180° while your pull his arm.

5. As you step back with your left foot rotate your body and press his hand down to the ground.

5

4

Long Stick Defense
Technique 3

1. Attacker has a staff in his hands. You are both in an open stance. You have your right leg back. Attacker has his left leg back. ***Dun-Ji-Gi***

2. Attacker strikes down at you while advancing with his right leg. Step forward with you left foot. Grab the staff directly over your head with your left hand. Your grip has your thumb pointing towards attacker.

3. Grab the staff between his grip with your right hand. As you pull attacker forwards, bring the staff over your head.

4. Step counter-clockwise with your left foot to face same direction as attacker. Continue rotating the staff in a circular motion.

5. Follow through to the ground. This motion will finish the staff striking the attacker's head.

1

Long Stick Defense Technique 4

1. Attacker has a staff in his hands. Both of you have your right legs back. ***Pal-Kum-Chi***
2. Attacker thrusts at you while stepping forward with his left foot. Step back with your left foot grabbing the end of the staff with your left hand.
3. Pull attacker towards you while grabbing the staff behind his left elbow with your right hand.
4. Pivot counter-clockwise on your right foot pulling the end of the staff with you. Push your right arm against attacker's elbow.
5. Continue forcing the attacker's elbow by leaning your body behind the push of your right arm. Attacker will finish on the ground.

2

5

3

4

SHORT STICK TECHNIQUES

Short Stick Technique 1

1. You are facing your attacker with a short stick in your right hand.

2. Attacker throws a right hand punch that you block with open left hand. Thrust your stick to attacker's solar plexus.

3. Bring the stick under and back over attacker's right punch. Your wrists are against each other forming a cross hold.

4. Grab the stick (fingers over) with your left hand. Flex your wrists over attacker's wrist as you bring your hands down on front of your belt. The attacker will fall to the ground in front of you.

Short Stick Technique 2

1. You are facing your attacker with a short stick in your right hand.

2. Attacker throws a right hand punch that you grab in a crane block. Your stick comes from your body parallel to the ground. Strike attacker's ribs by swinging it outward parallel to the ground.

3. In a circular motion bring the end of the stick over the outside of the attacker's right shoulder and back across his throat.

4. Continue the circular motion towards ground by stepping into the attacker with your right leg. The attacker once on the ground has a stick driving against his throat and his elbow is being hyper extended against your right hand hold. You aid this by pulling his arm against your right hold with your left hand. Pressure will increase on both areas.

Short Stick Technique 3

1. You are facing your attacker with a short stick in your right hand.

2. Attacker throws a right hand punch that you grab in a crane block. Your stick comes across your body parallel to the ground.

3. Strike attacker's ribs by swinging it outward parallel to the ground.

4. Attack the groin by dropping your stick down between attacker's legs swinging upward.

5. Drop to your right knee as you turn your stick parallel to the ground. This turn will push the stick against attacker's left leg and pull the stick against the back of attacker's right leg. The attacker will fall to the ground away from you.

5

4

Short Stick Technique 4

1. You are facing your attacker with a short stick in your right hand.

2. Attacker throws a right hand punch that you grab in a crane block. Your stick comes across your body parallel to the ground. Strike the attacker's ribs by swinging it outward parallel to the ground.

3. Step forward and to the side with your right leg bringing attacker's right hand, in circular motion, down and in front of you. Place your stick against attacker's right under arm.

1

2

3

4. Step forward with your left foot and pivot clockwise on both feet. Continue the circular motion by bringing attacker's right hand directly over your head and dropping to your left knee. The stick is used to lever the attacker's arm through the motion.

5. Following through in the same manner will bring the attacker to the ground in front of you.

6. Once on the ground, slip the stick from under attacker's arm to across his neck. With your left arm pull the attacker's arm against the stick increasing the pressure on his throat.

Double jumping kick

2 PERSON SELF-DEFENSE

2 PERSON SELF DEFENSE

Technique 1

1. Attacker #1 grabs(fingers over) your right lapel with his left hand. Attacker #2 grabs(thumb over) your left wrist with his right hand.

2. Step forward with your right foot. Grab(thumb over) attacker #1's left hand with your right hand. Make a circular motion inside out with your left hand to grab(fingers over) attacker #2"s right wrist.

3. Bring your elbow over attacker #1's left arm. Bend down on top of his elbow. Lift his left wrist skyward to bend sideways in the direction of his little finger.

2 PERSON SELF DEFENSE

4. Step in with your left foot as you swing attacker #2's right hand in a circular motion forward.

5. Pivot clockwise bringing attacker #2's hand over your head. The hold on attacker #1 is maintained throughout. With your left hand you will bend attacker #2's wrist back over his shoulder.

6. Both attackers will be on the ground and pressure can be maintained on both holds.

Technique 2

1. Attacker #1 grabs your right wrist with his right hand. Attacker #2 grabs your left wrist with his left hand.

2. In a circular motion turn your right hand inside out to grab(fingers over) attacker #1's right wrist. With the same motion grab attacker #2's left wrist. These are both done at the same time. Ensure that you bend attacker #2's left elbow by applying pressure over his wrist and straight down. Deliver a right leg side kick to attacker #1's mid section.

3. Pivot counter-clockwise on your left leg to place your right foot down behind attacker #2's left arm. Straighten his arm and deliver straight pressure against his elbow with your right hand.

4. Once on the ground, pin attacker with right knee and continue to apply pressure on his elbow.

Technique 3

1. Attacker #1 grabs your right wrist with his right hand. Attacker #2 grabs your left wrist with his left hand.

2. Stepping strongly with your left foot, push your arms bent and high. Your fingers are skyward. Your hands are between both holds.

3. Your hands will push outwards slightly against attacker's wrists. This will bend the wrists at the proper angle required for the technique. Grab (fingers over) attackers wrists.

4. Apply pressure straight downward to bend attacker's wrist painfully side-ways.

1

2

3

4

Tecnique 4

1. Attacker #1 grabs your right wrist with his right hand. Attacker #2 grabs your left wrist with his left hand.

2. Step forward with your left leg. Spin your thumbs outwards until your palms are against attacker's palms. Grab attacker #1's hand. Turn your right hand counter-clockwise as you lift attacker #1's hand under his right elbow. Lift attacker #2 's hand high. Increase the bend in his wrist as it rises.

3. Pivot clockwise on your left foot as you advance forward with your right foot. Attacker #2's arm will cross over attacker #1's arm. Continue to rotate attacker #2's arm counter-clockwise. Rotate attacker #1's arm clockwise.

2 PERSON SELF DEFENSE

4. Place attacker's elbows together. Bend attacker #1's arm upward. Bend attacker #2's arm downward.

5. Rotate both arms counter-clockwise.

6. This will rotate attacker #1's shoulder backward causing him to fall. This motion will also twist attacker #2's arm behind his back causing him to fall on top of attacker #1.

6

5

4

Breaking bricks with knife hand

WOMAN SELF-DEFENSE

Technique 1

1. Attacker grabs your purse from behind as it is slung over your shoulder.

2. Turn to your right immediately grabbing (thumb over) attacker's right hand with your right hand.

3. Pivot clockwise on both feet to face attacker squarely. This pivot, in combination with a cross thumb hold, will rotate attacker's right arm clockwise. Bend the wrist over with your grip.

4. Deliver a front kick to attackers mid section.

Tcchniquc 2

1. Attacker reaches to grab you with both his hands. You are holding an umbrella in your right hand.

2. Grab attacker's reaching left hand with a crane block. Your right hand comes up to your left shoulder. Strike attacker on the right side of his head by following his right arm with the swing of your umbrella.

3. Reach under and back over attacker's right arm with your umbrella so that it is positioned across attacker's wrist and parallel to the ground.

4. Release your left-hand hold to grab the other end of your umbrella locking attacker's arm in the triangle you have created. Apply downward pressure with the umbrella while pushing over and down with your arms until attacker is down.

1

Technique 3

1. You are holding your wallet in your right hand. Attacker grabs your right wrist with his left hand. He then tries to take your wallet with his right hand.

2. Grab (thumb over) his left wrist with your left hand. Step forward and to your right with your right foot.

3. Step forward with your left foot lifting attacker's arm in a circular motion high in front of you.

2

3

4. Pull your right hand out and place on attacker's left elbow. Apply pressure against his elbow until attacker is on the ground. Pull in opposite direction with your left hand.

5. Pivot clockwise on both your feet. Bring attacker's arm over your head keeping his elbow straight.

5

4

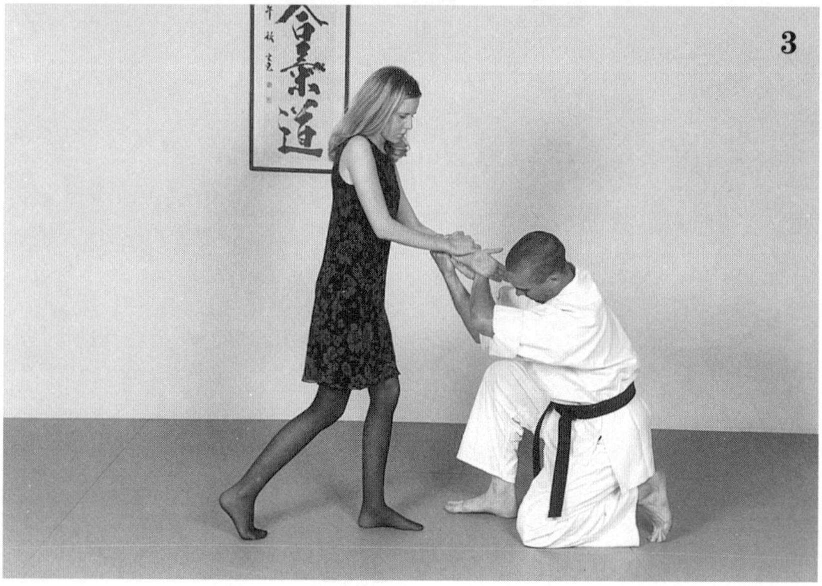

Technique 4

1. Attacker approaches you from behind. Attacker grabs your left wrist with both his hands.
2. Step back towards attacker with your left foot. Pivot strongly, bending your left elbow. Ensure your left hand is open and over attacker's left wrist.
3. Place your right hand(fingers over) on attacker's left fingers to prevent him from releasing his hold on your wrist. Begin applying pressure over and downward. On the attacker's left wrist by extending your left arm. Assist the action by leaning forward.